AF270074

Let's Learn American Sign Language

FEELINGS

Raymie Davis

Illustrations By:
Brad Manker,
35 Corks Art Studio

PowerKiDS
press

PK
Beginners

I can sign
about my feelings.
I use my hands.

happy

5

sad

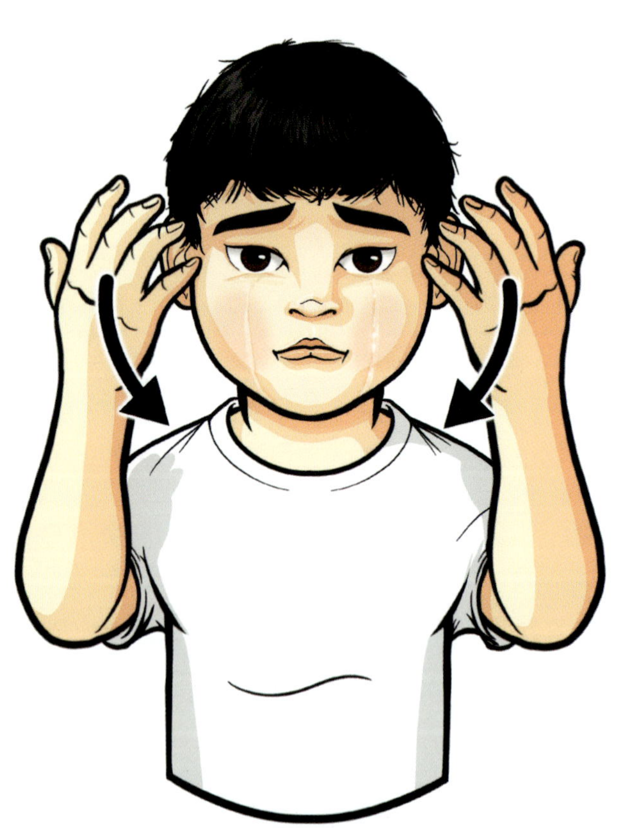

mad

9

scared

11

shy

tired

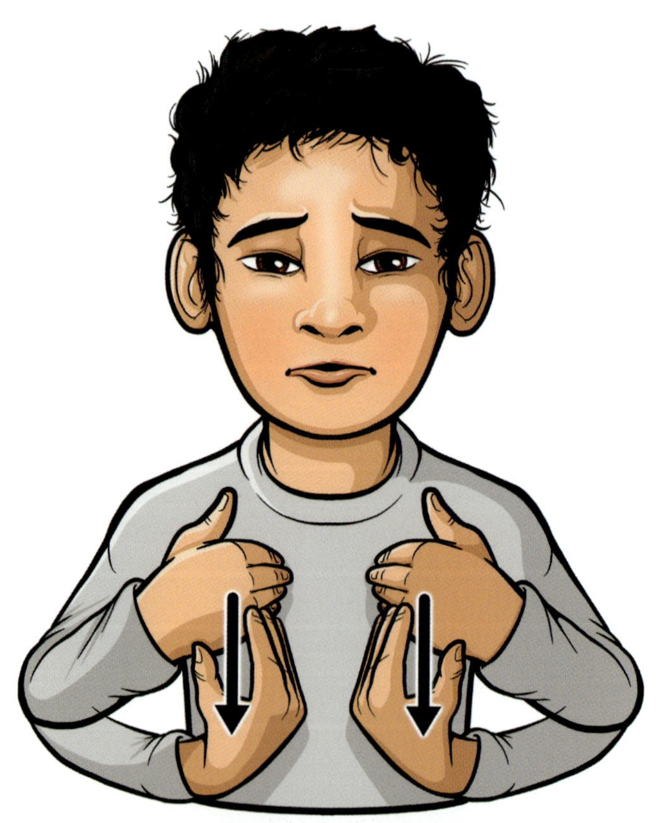

15

silly

17

excited

19

love

21

proud

22

23

Published in 2025 by The Rosen Publishing Group, Inc.
2544 Clinton Street, Buffalo, NY 14224

First Edition

Special thanks to Michelle Rose, M.S., American Sign Language Consultant

Book Design: Tanya Dellaccio Keeney
Illustrator: Brad Manker, 35 Corks Art Studio

Photo Credits: Cover (background pattern) Olgastocker/Shutterstock.com; cover (boy) New Africa/Shutterstock.com; p. 3 TimeImage Production/Shutterstock.com; p. 5 Kristina Igumnova26/Shutterstock.com; p. 7 anut21ng Stock/Shutterstock.com; p. 9 Monkey Business Images/Shutterstock.com; p. 11 Roman Samborskyi/Shutterstock.com; p. 13 UfaBizPhoto/Shutterstock.com; p. 15 airdone/Shutterstock.com; p. 17 PinkCoffee Studio/Shutterstock.com; p. 19 oes/Shutterstock.com; p. 21 fizkes/Shutterstock.com; p. 23 Anatoliy Karlyuk/Shutterstock.com.

Library of Congress Cataloging-in-Publication Data

Names: Davis, Raymie, author.
Title: Feelings / Raymie Davis.
Description: Buffalo, NY : PowerKids Press, [2025] | Series: Let's learn
    American Sign Language
Identifiers: LCCN 2023036668 (print) | LCCN 2023036669 (ebook) | ISBN
    9781499443516 (library binding) | ISBN 9781499443509 (paperback) | ISBN
    9781499443523 (ebook)
Subjects: LCSH: American Sign Language--Juvenile literature. |
    Emotions--Juvenile literature. | Social learning--Juvenile literature.
Classification: LCC HV2476.4 .D38 2025 (print) | LCC HV2476.4 (ebook) |
    DDC 419/.7--dc23/eng/20230831
LC record available at https://lccn.loc.gov/2023036668
LC ebook record available at https://lccn.loc.gov/2023036669

Manufactured in the United States of America

CPSIA Compliance Information: Batch #CSPK25. For further information contact Rosen Publishing at 1-800-237-9932.

Find us on